SIGNIN FUN

American Sign Language
Vocabulary, Phrases, Games,
& Activities

Penny Warner

Illustrations by Paula Gray

Clerc Books • Gallaudet University Press
Washington, D.C.

Gallaudet University Press
Washington, DC 20002
http://gupress.gallaudet.edu

© 2006 by Gallaudet University
All rights reserved. Published 2006
Printed in the United States of America

16 15 14 13 12 11 10 09 08 07   2 3 4 5 6 7 8 9

Library of Congress Cataloging-in-Publication Data

Warner, Penny.
    Signing fun : American Sign Language vocabulary, phrases, games &
activities / Penny Warner ; illustrations by Paula Gray.
        p. cm.
    Includes index.
    ISBN-10 1-56368-292-3 (alk. paper); ISBN-13 978-1-56368-292-6 (alk. paper)
    1. American Sign Language—Juvenile literature.   2. American Sign Language—Vocabulary—
Juvenile literature.   3. American Sign Language Conversation and phrase books—Juvenile
literature.   I. Gray, Paula, ill.   II. Title.
HV2476.W37 2006
419′.7—dc22

                                                                                2006041269

∞ The paper used in this publication meets the minimum requirements of American National
Standard for Information Sciences—Permanence of Paper for Printed Library Materials, ANSI
Z39.48.1984.

Contents

Introduction

Kids love sign language! That's because it's visual, it's fun, and it's easy to learn. Students who know American Sign Language (ASL) use it to share secrets in silence with special friends.

American Sign Language is the fourth most commonly used language in the United States. Many colleges and universities now accept ASL to fulfill their foreign language requirement. Learning ASL can help students reinforce vocabulary, strengthen language skills, improve spelling, and increase reading ability. It can even lead to job opportunities, such as teaching or interpreting for deaf students.

Signing Fun: American Sign Language Vocabulary, Phrases, Games, & Activities offers a wide variety of signs on kids' favorite topics, including animals, emotions, fashion, food, holidays, home, outdoors, parties, people, places, school, shopping, sports, and travel. Each chapter ends with sample sentences so that students can practice the newly learned signs in a fun way. Helpful tips for signing, such as where to place the hands and how to choose a name sign, are scattered throughout the book. The book also offers dozens of entertaining games and activities to play with ASL, such as Alphabet Sign, Finger Fun, Gesture Guess, Match Signs, Mime and Sign, Oppo-Sign, Picture Hand, Secret Sign, Sign-A-Gories, Signo Bingo, Snap and Sign, and Sign or Dare.

HOW TO MAKE SIGNS

All signs have three basic parts: the shape of the hand (handshape), the place where the sign is made, and the way the hand moves. Each sign in this book includes a description of how to make the sign. The handshapes in ASL come from the American Manual Alphabet (chapter 1), the manual numbers (chapter 2), and variations of these shapes (see the chart on page ix).

The hand you write with is called your *dominant* hand. You should use your dominant hand when you fingerspell and make one-hand signs. For most people, this is the right hand. When a sign uses both hands, your right hand will make most of the movements and your left hand will act as a base. Many of the sign descriptions in this book do not specify which hand to use, so you should use your dominant hand. Sometimes, the descriptions do explain which hand to use, and these directions are written for right-handed signers. If you are left-handed, substitute "left" for "right" in the sign directions.

Now you are ready to get started. First, you will learn the manual alphabet and the manual numbers. Learning to sign is just plain fun. So get your fingers ready and let's begin!

SPECIAL HANDSHAPES

Open A   Open B   Bent B   Baby O

Flat O   Bent V   Bent 5   Open 8

SIGNING
FUN

1

THE AMERICAN MANUAL ALPHABET

Signers use the American Manual Alphabet to spell English words that don't have signs. This is called *fingerspelling*. Each handshape represents a different letter of the English alphabet. Once you learn the alphabet, you will be able to finger-spell any word.

AMERICAN MANUAL ALPHABET

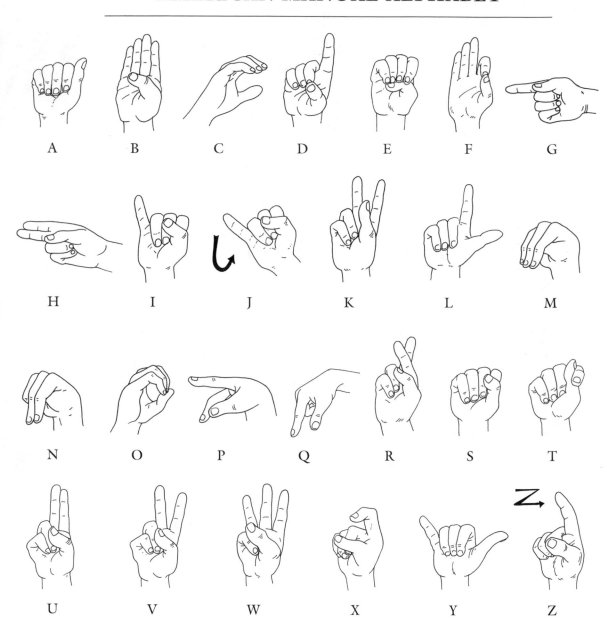

A   B   C   D   E   F   G

H   I   J   K   L   M

N   O   P   Q   R   S   T

U   V   W   X   Y   Z

2

THE MANUAL NUMBERS

You can use the manual numbers to sign any number you can think of. A few of the number handshapes look like the number they represent—1, 2, 4, and 5. The rest of the number handshapes do not, so pay attention!

The following numbers are shown with the palm facing outward so you can see them clearly. However, when you sign 1, 2, 3, 4, and 5, your palm should face your body.

Now, turn your palm outward to sign 6, 7, 8, and 9. When you sign 10, your palm faces left and you shake your hand side-to-side a little.

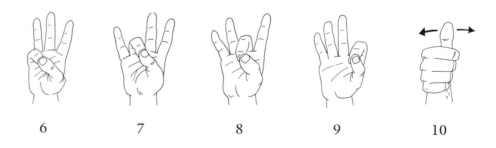

HELPFUL HINTS
FOR SIGNING NUMBERS

To sign your phone number, sign each number individually.
For example, *837-7089* is signed "8-3-7-7-0-8-9."

Sign each number in your address individually. For example,
710 Adams Place is signed as "7-1-0," not "7-10."

To sign your age, sign **age** at your chin, move your
hand forward, and sign the number.

Sign dollar amounts the way you would say them.
For example, *$10.59* is signed "ten fifty-nine."

Sign years as you would say them. For example,
1989 is signed "nineteen eighty-nine."

Make the next group of numbers with your palm facing your body. When you sign 11 and 12, you flick your fingers up twice. When you sign 13, 14, and 15, you bend your fingers down twice.

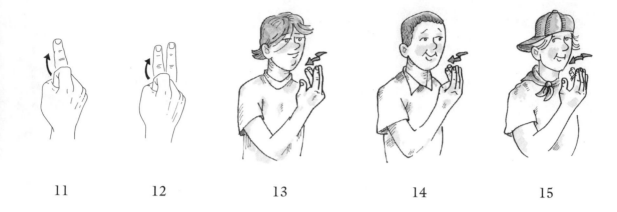

11   12   13   14   15

The signs for 16 through 19 have two parts. First, you make the number 10 and then you twist your hand out and sign the second number (6, 7, 8, or 9).

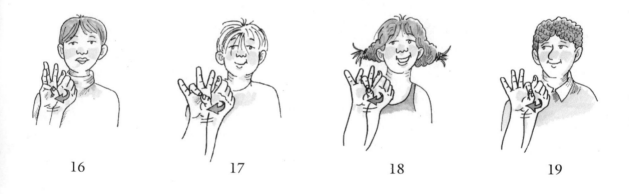

16   17   18   19

Most of the signs for two-digit numbers follow the same pattern—sign the first number and then the second number. The signs for 20–29 are an exception to this rule. Instead of signing 2, you begin with a modified L handshape. To sign 20, make the L and then tap your index fingertip on your thumb twice, like this:

20

To sign 21, turn the L sideways, so your thumb is sticking up, and bend your thumb up and down. For 22, you use the 2 hand-shape, but the palm faces down. Then you bounce your hand to the right. For 23, make a 3 and bend your middle finger a couple of times. To sign 24, make the L and then 4. The sign for 25 is similar to the sign 23; start with 5 and then bend your middle finger several times. To sign 26–29, make an L and then the appropriate number.

| 21 | 22 | 23 | 24 | 25 |

To count from 30 to 90 by tens, start with the initial number and add 0. To sign the numbers in between, make both numbers. For example, 31 is a combination of 3 and 1.

30   40   50   60

70   80   90

The sign for 100 is 1 plus C. The sign for 1000 starts with a 1 and then you place your right fingertips in your left palm.

100   1000

3

JUST DO IT!
Activity Signs

Activity signs are easy to learn. Many of the signs for sports and activities resemble the actual sport or game. It's time to "play" with signs!

9

play

Hold Y hands in front of your chest and shake them back and forth.

sports/competition

Put 10 hands together with knuckles touching and twist hands back and forth.

game

Bring 10 hands together and knock knuckles together.

swim

Turn your hands palms face down, then move them apart as if you are swimming the breaststroke.

skate

Turn Bent V hands palms up; move them alternately back and forth, as if skating.

ski/skiing

Turn X hands palms up and move them forward twice.

skateboard

Place an upside-down U hand on the back of your other hand and zigzag the hands forward.

horseback ride

Place an upside-down V hand on a sideways B hand and bounce both hands forward.

basketball

Hold 3 hands up and wiggle them.

soccer

Use a B hand to kick the side of your other hand.

SIGNING TIPS

Hold your hand with your palm facing out so the other person can see your signs clearly.

Keep your hand and arm relaxed so you won't get tired while you sign.

Keep your hand steady so your words and letters don't bounce.

---

baseball

Place one S hand on top of the other; hold hands up by your shoulder (as if you are holding a bat), and move the hands back and forth twice.

hockey

Brush the index finger of an X hand along your other palm twice.

football

Bring 5 hands together, interlocking them twice to make football "laces."

gymnastics

Place the left H hand across the wrist of the right H hand, palm out. Twist the right hand down and around, ending with the palm facing in.

computer

Place your C hand near your shoulder, then bounce your hand down your arm.

Internet

Place middle fingers of Open 8 hands together, move hands in a circle, tapping middle fingers together.

cards/deal cards

Move one Baby O hand like you are dealing cards, but leave the other one still.

music/sing/song

Wave your right hand back and forth over your left forearm.

guitar

Hold the neck of a guitar with your left A hand, and strum the guitar with your right A hand.

drum

Take turns beating a drum with two Baby O hands.

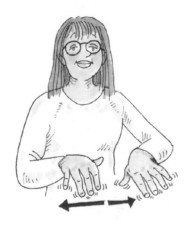

keyboard/piano

Wiggle your fingers along an imaginary keyboard.

dance

Swing an upside-down V hand over the open palm.

telephone/cell phone

Place a Y hand on your cheek, as if you are talking on a telephone.

Walkman/radio

Place Bent 5 hands over your ears.

movie

Put palms of 5 hands together and twist your right hand from side to side.

videotape

Place a V hand on top of the fingertips of your other hand, move the V forward in a circle and end with a T hand on your palm.

TV
Fingerspell T-V.

watch
Point the fingers of the V hand out and move your hand forward.

PRACTICE SENTENCES

1. **Let's go play.**

you-and-me

play

2. What do you want to play?

what   play   you

3. Call me (on the phone).

telephone   me

4. Let's watch TV.

you-and-me   watch   TV

5. Do you want to play video games?

you   want   play   video   game

6. I won!

me   win

4

LIONS, TIGERS, AND BEARS, OH MY!
Animal Signs

Animal signs are easy to learn. For most you just act like the animal!

animal

Place fingertips of bent hands on chest, bend fingers down and up on your chest twice.

cat

Pull a "whisker" from the side of your mouth.

dog

Pat your leg, then snap your finger, as if calling your dog.

horse

Place the thumb with U fingers extended at the side of your forehead and bend fingers down.

cow

Place the thumb of your Y hand at the side of your forehead to form a horn, then twist your hand back a little.

bird

Place a G hand next to your chin; open and close your thumb and index finger to make a bird's beak.

frog

Place an S hand under your chin and flick V fingers twice.

fish

Place the fingertips of your right hand against your left wrist, then wiggle your right hand forward, like a fish swimming.

rabbit

Cross U hands on your upper chest and bend the fingers down twice.

deer

Place both 5 hands on your temples.

sheep

Open and close the fingers of the right V hand, palm up, while moving your hand up the back of your other arm, as if shearing a sheep.

chicken

Open and close the thumb and index finger of a G hand at the side of your chin, then peck at your other palm with a closed G.

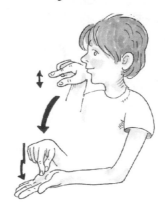

skunk

Place a K hand on top of your head and move your hand back to show a skunk's white stripe.

snake

Move a Bent V hand from your chin outward in a zigzag motion.

monkey

Scratch the sides of your trunk with both Bent 5 hands.

owl

Place O hands over your eyes, then bend your wrists up and down twice.

squirrel

Put Bent V hands together, then tap fingertips against each other twice.

bee

Touch your cheek with your index finger, then brush your cheek with a B hand, as if brushing away a bee.

butterfly

Cross 5 hands with thumbs hooked and wiggle your fingers.

bug

Place the thumb of a 3 hand on your nose, then bend your index and middle fingers twice.

bear

Cross Bent 5 hands on your chest and open and close your fingers like you are scratching.

tiger

Place Bent 5 hands over your face, then pull them apart twice.

lion

Slide a Bent 5 hand over your head to show the lion's mane.

zoo

Draw a Z with your index finger on your other palm.

PRACTICE SENTENCES

1. Do you have a cat?

you

have

cat

2. Let's go to the zoo.

you-and-me

go

zoo

3. I love animals.

me

love

animal

4. Where's the dog food?

where

dog

food

5. I want a horse.

me

want

horse

6. I saw a beautiful butterfly.

me

saw

beautiful

butterfly

5

WHEN YOU GROW UP
Career Signs

Here are some signs to help you decide what you want to be when you grow up. First you will learn the sign for **person**. Then you can add it to almost any other sign and be anything you want to be.

person

Move flat hands down the sides of your chest.

lawyer (law + person)

Move an L down your palm then sign **person**.

doctor

Tap a D on your upturned wrist (you don't have to sign **person**).

nurse

Tap an N on your upturned wrist (you don't have to sign **person**).

artist (art + person)
Wiggle the pinky of an I hand down your palm, as if drawing, then sign **person**.

singer/musician
(music + person)
Wave an Open B hand inside your other arm, then sign **person**.

actor (act + person)
Move A hands alternately in circles toward your chest, then sign **person**.

dancer
(dance + person)
Swing an upside-down V over your upturned palm, then sign **person**.

police officer

Tap a C hand below your opposite shoulder, where a badge would be (you don't have to sign **person**).

firefighter

Tap the back of the B hand against your forehead (you don't have to sign **person**).

postal carrier
(letter + person)

Lick your thumb, place it on your open palm, and sign **person**.

airline pilot
(airplane + person)

Extend your thumb, index finger, and pinky and move your hand forward in two quick motions; then sign **person**.

scientist
(science + person)

Turn A hands upside down and circle them alternately, as if mixing chemicals, then sign **person**.

cook/chef
(cook + person)

Place an Open B hand down on your other palm, then flip your hand over, as if turning a pancake; then sign **person**.

SIGNING TIPS

If you are asking a question, raise your eyebrows and tilt your head forward. You can also add a question mark at the end of a sentence by drawing the mark with your index finger.

Keep your mouth visible so the other person can read your lips.

---

clown

Place a Bent 5 hand over your nose to make a clown nose (you don't have to sign **person**).

magician
(magic + person)

Pull S hands back slightly and then throw them forward while opening your hands; then sign **person**.

librarian
(library + person)

Circle an L hand in the air and then sign **person**.

veterinarian

Spell V-E-T.

waiter/server
(serve + person)

Slide Open B hands, palms up, from side to side, as if moving a tray, then sign **person**.

interpreter
(interpret + person)

Bring the thumb and index fingers of both F hands together at an angle, twist hands in opposite directions, and then sign **person**.

soldier

Place one A hand under your shoulder and the other A hand on your abdomen, as if holding a rifle (you don't have to sign **person**).

teacher
(teach + person)

Move Flat O hands out from forehead and then sign **person**.

secretary

Swing a Baby O hand from behind your ear down to slide off your palm, as if writing a note (you don't have to sign **person**).

president

Place C hands at your forehead and move them out while closing them (you don't have to sign **person**).

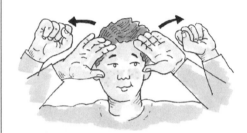

PRACTICE SENTENCES

1. What do you want to be when you grow up?

| what | you | want | work |

2. My mother is a teacher.

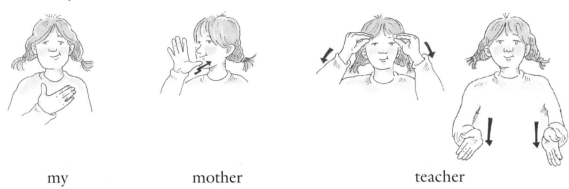

my   mother   teacher

3. My father is a clown.

my   father   clown

4. I want to be an interpreter.

me   want   interpreter

6

ROSES ARE RED, VIOLETS ARE BLUE
Color Signs

You can make a rainbow of colors once you learn these signs.

red

Slide your index finger down your lips, ending with an X hand.

orange

Squeeze an O hand at your mouth.

yellow

Twist a Y hand in front of your shoulder.

purple

Twist a P hand in front of your shoulder.

blue

Twist a B hand in front of your shoulder.

green

Twist a G hand in front of your shoulder.

brown

Slide a B hand down your cheek.

black

Wipe an index finger across your forehead.

pink

Brush a P hand down your lips.

white

Place a Bent 5 hand on your chest, then pull it out while changing to a Flat O hand.

tan

Slide a T hand down your cheek.

gray

Brush the fingers of your 5 hands back and forth between each other.

rainbow

Sign **color**, then arc a 4 hand across the top of your head.

color

Place the fingers of a 4 hand on your chin and wiggle your fingers.

PRACTICE SENTENCES

1. What color is that?

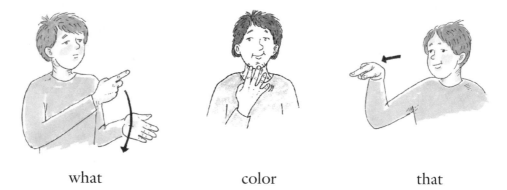

what · color · that

ROSES ARE RED, VIOLETS ARE BLUE

2. What's your favorite color?

what favorite color you

3. My favorite color is _____.

my favorite color (sign your favorite color)

4. There's a rainbow.

there rainbow

7

STYLIN'
Clothing and
Fashion Signs

Practice these clothing and fashion signs and you'll soon be stylin'.

clothes/dress

Brush the thumbs of your Open B hands down your chest twice.

shirt

Pinch the fabric of your shirt and tug on it twice.

wear

Brush the thumbs of your Open B hands down your chest.

pants

Place B hands on your thighs, pull them up, and close them to Flat O hands at your waist.

shorts

Slide Bent B hands across your thighs twice, as if showing the length of your shorts.

pajamas

Start with a 4 hand on your forehead, pull it down to a Flat O at your chin, and then sign **clothes**.

jacket/coat

Place A hands on upper chest, smooth them down to your waist, as if pulling on a coat.

underwear

Place one 5 hand above the other 5 hand and brush the lower hand down twice.

socks

Place index fingers together, pointing down, and slide them alternately back and forth.

shoes

Tap S hands together.

clean

Slide one Open B hand along the palm of the other Open B hand.

dirty

Place a 5 hand under your chin and wiggle your fingers.

ring

Rock an F hand on your ring finger.

bracelet

Grip an index finger and thumb around your wrist and twist.

earring

Pinch an earlobe with an F hand.

necklace

Place index fingers below your neck and circle fingers up to your neck to form a necklace.

watch

Place an F hand on the back of your wrist.

ugly

Slide an index finger under your nose and change to an X hand.

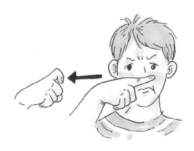

cute

Brush a U hand down your chin twice, ending with bent fingers.

PRACTICE SENTENCES

1. What are you wearing?

what   you   wear

2. Your shirt is cute!

you   shirt   cute

3. I love those shoes!

me   love   those   shoes

4. My pajamas are dirty.

my   pajamas   dirty

8

MAD, SAD, AND GLAD
Feeling Signs

You can show your feelings by using facial expressions when you sign.

feel

Brush the middle finger of your 5 hand up your chest twice.

happy

Brush an Open B hand up your chest twice.

sad

Hold 5 hands over your eyes, then move the hands down your face.

mad

Place Bent 5 hands over your abdomen, then sharply raise your hands up.

love
Cross S hands on your chest.

I love you
Hold out your hand with the thumb, index finger, and pinky extended.

hate
Flick open the middle fingers of 8 hands.

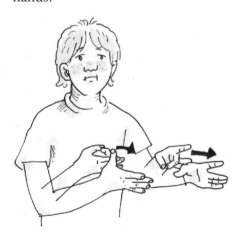

afraid
Hold A hands below your shoulders, then move them toward each other while flicking open your hands.

excited

Alternate brushing the middle fingers of Open 8 hands up your chest twice.

mean

Place one Bent 5 hand near your chin and the other near your waist; then move your hands toward and past each other as you close them to fists.

SIGNING TIPS

Keep your face visible so the other person
can see your facial expressions.

If you are saying something negative,
shake your head and frown.

If you are excited about something, smile!

embarrassed

Hold 5 hands near your chin, palms in, then move your hands alternately up and down over your face, as if showing how it fills with color.

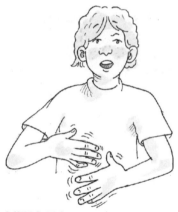

nervous

Hold 5 hands in front of your chest and shake them as if you are nervous.

shy

Place the knuckles of a Bent B hand on your cheek, twist your hand forward until the thumb is pointing up.

jealous

Place your pinky finger at the side of your mouth, then make a J.

surprise

Hold Baby O hands at your temples and flick open your index fingers.

sorry/apologize

Circle an A hand on your chest.

tired

Place the fingertips of Bent B hands on your chest, then twist your hands down onto your chest.

lonely

Place an index finger on your lips and brush your finger down the middle of your chin.

bored

Twist an index finger on the side of your nose.

curious

Place an F hand on the middle of your neck and give a little twist.

good

Move a B hand down from your lips so it lands in your other palm.

bad

Begin with the fingertips of a B hand at your lips, then twist your hand out and down.

PRACTICE SENTENCES

1. How are you feeling?

how   you   feel

2. I'm happy.

me   happy

3. I love you.

me   love   you

4. I hate that.

me   hate   that

5. I feel good.

me   feel   good

6. I'm sorry you feel bad.

me   sorry   you   feel   bad

9

TIME TO EAT!
Food Signs

Learn the signs for different foods, then ask for a snack or drink.

food/eat

Tap a Flat O hand on your mouth twice.

hungry

Place the fingers of your C hand below your neck and slide your hand down your chest.

thirsty

Slide an index finger down your neck.

breakfast

Sign **eat** and then sign **morning**.

dinner

Sign **eat** and then sign **night**.

lunch

Sign **eat** and then sign **noon**.

meat

Pinch the skin between your thumb and index finger.

bread

Slice the back of an Open B hand with a Bent B hand several times.

hamburger

Place C hands together, as if shaping a hamburger, then open and reverse the hand positions.

french fries

Bounce an F hand twice to the side.

hot dog

Hold C hands together, then open and close them as you move the hands apart.

cookie

Place a C hand on your palm and twist it, as if using a cookie cutter.

ice cream

Pretend to hold an ice cream cone at your mouth and brush it against your chin twice.

water

Tap a W hand on your chin twice.

milk

Squeeze an O hand several times.

chocolate

Circle a C on the back of your other hand.

popcorn

Place S hands in front of your chest, then alternate flicking up your index fingers several times.

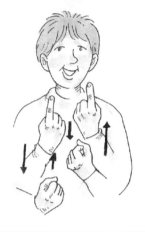

bacon

Hold N hands in front of your chest and wiggle them apart.

egg

Put your right H fingers on top of your left H fingers, then move the hands apart as if breaking an egg.

peanut butter

Sign P + B.

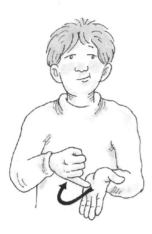

jelly

Brush a J on your palm twice.

apple

Twist an X hand on your cheek.

cheese

Place heels of palms together with fingers facing opposite directions and twist hands.

banana

Peel your left index finger with your right Baby O hand twice.

fruit

Twist an F hand back and forth on your cheek.

___

cup/glass

Tap a C hand on your palm.

vegetable

Place the index finger of a V hand on your cheek, then twist your hand back and forth.

___

plate

Make a plate-sized circle with your thumbs and index fingers.

fork

Tap an upside-down V hand on your palm.

knife

Place your right H fingers on top of your left H fingers and sharply slice your right H off your left hand.

spoon

Place an H hand on your palm, lift your hand toward your mouth twice.

PRACTICE SENTENCES

1. I'm hungry.

me

hunger

2. Are you thirsty?

you

thirsty

3. I want breakfast.

me

want

breakfast

4. What's for dinner?

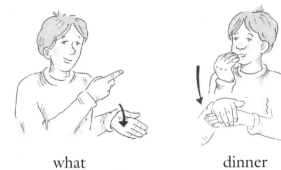

what   dinner

5. I love chocolate ice cream.

me   love   chocolate   ice cream

6. Do you want more french fries?

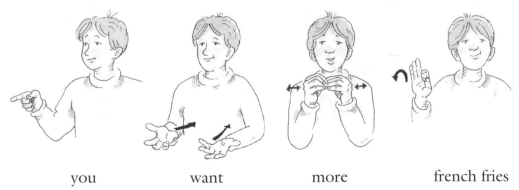

you   want   more   french fries

10

FEELING GOOD
Health Signs

If you have an emergency, or just don't feel well, learn these signs so you can tell the doctor what's wrong!

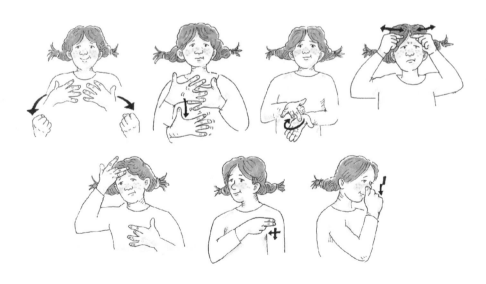

healthy

Put both 5 hands on your chest, then pull them out while closing to S hands.

sick

Place the middle finger of your right Open 8 hand on your forehead and the middle finger of your left Open 8 hand on your chest.

hurt/pain

Point index fingers toward each other in front of your chest, then move your hands in and out twice.

tummyache

Place your index fingers at your stomach and move them in and out twice.

headache

Place your index fingers at your forehead and move them in and out twice.

break/broken

Place S hands together, palms down, and break them apart.

blood

Place your right 5 hand on top of your left 5 hand, palms facing in, then move your right hand down while wiggling your fingers, like dripping blood.

cut

Slice across the back of an S hand with your index finger.

temperature/fever

Place your right horizontal index finger across your left upright index finger, then slide your right hand up and down.

pill

Flick the index finger of a Baby O hand at your mouth, as if popping in a pill.

medicine

Place the middle finger of an Open 8 hand in your palm and draw small circles.

shot

Put your index finger on your arm and bend your thumb and index finger, as if giving yourself a shot.

throw up/vomit

Hold 5 hands at your mouth, one hand below the other, then arc hands forward and down.

cold

Place a Baby O hand at your nose and move your hand down twice.

hospital

Draw a cross on your upper arm with an H hand.

operation

Place the thumb of an A hand on your chest and slice down and across to the other side.

PRACTICE SENTENCES

1. I feel sick!

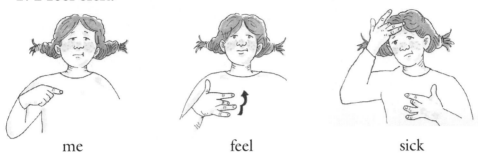

me   feel   sick

2. Call the doctor!

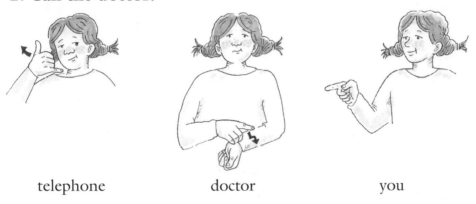

telephone   doctor   you

3. It hurts right here.

hurt (point to where it hurts)

4. I'm going to throw up!

me

throw up

11

CELEBRATE!
Holiday Signs

Celebrate your favorite holidays with fun and festive signs.

holiday/vacation

Place the thumbs of your 5 hands below your shoulders and tap your chest twice.

New Year's Eve

Scoop your right hand off your left palm, close both hands, and circle your hands around each other, ending with your right hand on top of your left hand; then sign **night**.

New Year's Day

Scoop your right hand off your left palm, close both hands, and circle your hands around each other, ending with your right hand on top of your left hand; then sign **day**.

Valentine's Day

Place your middle fingers on your heart and trace a heart on your chest; then sign **day**.

celebrate/anniversary

Circle Baby O hands above your shoulders.

sweetheart

Place 10 hands together over your heart and wiggle your thumbs up and down.

St. Patrick's Day

Brush an S hand down your other palm, then fingerspell P-A-T and sign **day**.

President's Day

Place C hands at your forehead and move them out while closing them; then sign **day**.

Easter

Hold an E hand facing out and twist it slightly.

Independence Day

Place I hands at your chin, swing them out and around, and sign **day**.

Passover

Move a P hand over the back of your other hand.

Halloween

Cover your eyes with H hands, then swing your hands back around to your temples.

Thanksgiving

Place the fingertips of both 5 hands near your mouth, then bounce your hands forward in two arcs.

SIGNING TIPS

When you talk about something that happened in the past, begin the sentence by waving your hand back over your shoulder.

When you are talking about something that will take place in the future, begin the sentence by moving your hand forward.

---

turkey

Wiggle a G hand below your chin.

Christmas

Begin with a C hand below your left shoulder, then flip your hand around in an arc.

Santa Claus

Place C hands at your chin and arc them down to your chest to form Santa's beard.

Hanukkah

Hold 4 hands out in front of your body, with index fingers close together, then move your hands out and up to form a menorah.

PRACTICE SENTENCES

1. We're going on vacation.

we   go   vacation

2. Happy holidays!

happy   holiday

3. Be my Valentine, sweetheart.

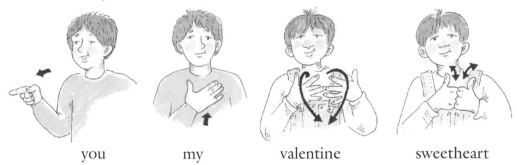

you   my   valentine   sweetheart

4. I love turkey!

me   love   turkey

5. Merry Christmas!

happy   Christmas

12

HOME
SWEET HOME
Home Signs

There are a dozen household signs right under your finger-tips.

home

Place the fingertips of a Flat O hand at your mouth, then move your hand back to the side of your face.

house

Form the roof and sides of a house with your hands.

door

Hold B hands together, palms out, and pull one hand back several times.

window

Place one B hand on top of the other B hand and lift the top hand, as if opening a window.

room/box

Hold Open B hands out, with palms facing, then turn hands in so one is in front of the other, as if shaping a box.

bed

Lay your cheek on your hands.

bedroom

Lay your cheek on one hand, then sign **room**.

---

blanket

Pretend to pull up a blanket with Flat O hands.

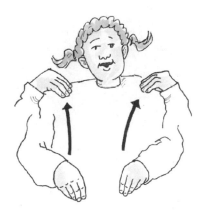

lamp

Set the elbow of a Flat O hand on your other palm, then open your hand.

alarm

Tap your palm with the index finger of your 1 hand.

poster

Outline a square with your index fingers.

curtain

Hold up 4 hands and bend them down twice.

closet

Hang an X hand on the index finger of your other hand and bounce the X down your index finger.

kitchen

Shake a K hand in the air.

refrigerator

Shake upright R hands in front of your chest.

bathroom/toilet

Shake a T hand in front of your chest.

mirror

Hold a hand up to your face and twist it twice.

bath

Rub A hands up and down on your chest, as if cleaning yourself.

shower

Hold an S hand over your head, and open and close your fingers, as if sprinkling yourself.

furniture

Shake an F hand in the air.

table/desk

Place one arm on top of the other arm and tap twice.

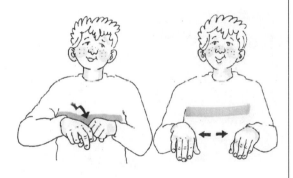

couch/sofa

Sign **chair**, then place C hands, palms down, in front of your body and move them apart.

chair

Bend your right H fingers on top of your left H hand and tap twice.

light/light bulb

Place an 8 hand under your chin, palm up, and flick open your middle finger several times.

picture

Place a C hand around your eye,
then bring it down to your other
hand.

PRACTICE SENTENCES

1. What color is your bedroom?

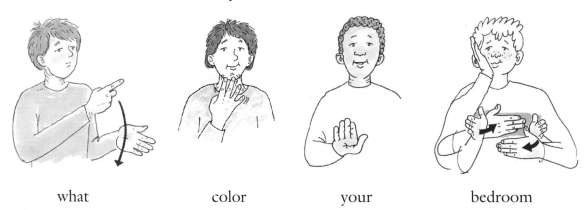

what   color   your   bedroom

2. This is my house.

this   my   house

3. I'm going home.

me   go   home

4. I need a shower.

me   need   shower

5. My computer is on my desk.

| my | computer | there | desk |

HOME SWEET HOME

13

HOW MUCH?
HOW MANY?
Measurement Signs

How do your signs measure up to our signs?

big/large

Hold L hands close together, then move them apart.

little/small

Hold Open B hands close together and move them closer.

high

Raise H hand upward.

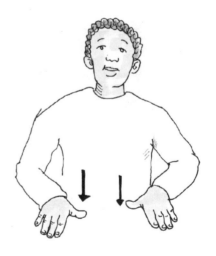

low

Push Open B hands down.

light (weight)

Start with Open 8 hands, palms down, then swing hands up and around.

heavy

Bounce Bent 5 hands down a little.

many

Place S hands in front of your chest, then drop your hands and open them.

how much/how many

Raise S hands and open your fingers.

few/several

Start with a Flat O hand, then slowly spread fingers.

enough

Place your right 5 hand on top of your left S hand, then brush the right hand forward.

SIGNING TIP

Use gestures and handshapes to show place
and size. If you are talking about an object nearby,
point to it. If you are talking about something
small, show the size with your hands.

---

far

Hold A hands together, then move one hand forward.

short

Lower a Bent B hand to show how short a person is.

close/near

Place one Bent B hand in front of the other Bent B hand, and tap the hands together twice.

tall

Raise a Bent B hand to show how tall a person is.

up
Point up with an index finger.

down
Point down with an index finger.

more
Tap the fingertips of Flat O hands together twice.

some/part/piece
Slide an Open B hand across your other palm toward you.

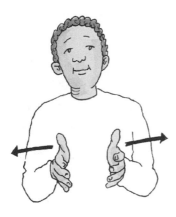

a lot/much

Hold Bent 5 hands in front of your chest, then arc them further apart.

nothing

Hold an S hand under your chin, then throw your hand forward and open your fingers.

something

Make small circles in the air with a 1 hand.

none

Place both O hands in front of your chest, then move your hands forward and out.

PRACTICE SENTENCES

1. How far is your house.

how   far   your   house

2. How many cats do you have?

how many   cats   you   have

3. I want a lot more.

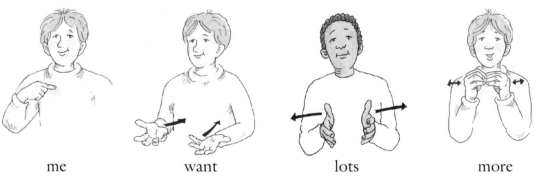

me   want   lots   more

4. May I have some?

me   have   some

5. How tall are you?

how   tall   you

14

GET GOING!
Movement Signs

If you want to see some action, keep those hands and fingers moving.

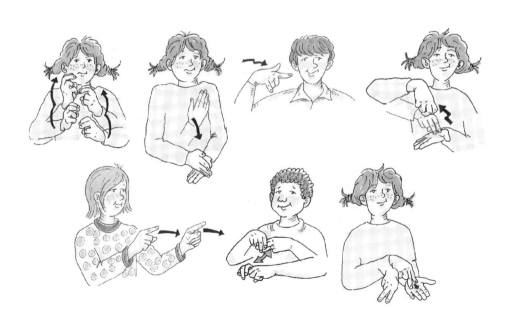

go

Point index fingers up, with palms out, then arc them forward.

come

Point index fingers out, with palms up, then arc them toward you.

stop

Bring the side of an Open B hand down onto your other palm.

move

Move Flat O hands from one side of your body to the other.

climb

Raise Bent V hands alternately above each other.

hit

Strike your index finger with an S hand.

miss

Move a C hand across your face and close it to an S hand.

hide

Place the thumb of an A hand on your chin, then tuck it under your other hand.

find/discover

Lift up a 5 hand and change it to an F hand, as if picking up something.

fly

Make an **I-love-you** hand and move it forward.

lose

Hold Flat O hands together, then drop them down as you open them.

make

Place one S hand on top of the other and twist the hands in opposite directions.

help

Place your right S hand on your left palm, and lift your hands.

Tap right Bent H fingers on left H fingers.

stand

Place an upside-down V hand on your other palm.

ride

Put Bent H fingers in a C hand and move your hands forward.

walk

Move Open B hands forward in alternating steps.

run

Place L hands together, with thumbs touching, and move hands forward while bending your index fingers.

jump

Put an upside-down V hand on your other palm, then lift your hand and bend your V fingers twice.

slide

Place an upside-down V hand on your other palm and slide your fingers off your palm.

swing

Sign **sit** and rock your hands back and forth.

leave

Quickly move a 5 hand out to the side while closing to a Flat O hand.

PRACTICE SENTENCES

1. **Sit down!**

sit-down

2. Did you lose your dog?

you   lose   dog   you

3. Let's leave today.

you-and-me   leave   today

4. Stand up!

stand-up

5. Let's make cookies.

you-and-me   make   cookie

6. Help me!

help   me

15

OUT & ABOUT
Outdoor Signs

Learn some signs about the great outdoors so you can talk about the weather, the seasons, and the planets.

weather

Wiggle a W hand down in front of
your chest.

sky

Move an Open B hand across the
top of your head.

sun

Tap a C hand on the side of your
face, near your eye.

moon

Tap an L hand, with index finger
bent, on the side of your face, near
your eye.

cloud

Hold both Bent 5 hands over one side of your head, then circle your hands around each other while moving across your head.

rain

Hold Bent 5 hands above your shoulders and bounce them down.

snow

Hold 5 hands above your shoulders and wiggle your fingers as you move your hands down in a zigzag pattern.

wind

Swing 5 hands back and forth in front of your chest.

stars

Brush upright index fingers
against each other twice.

dark

Place Open B hands on either side
of your face, palms in, then move
them down and end with wrists
crossed.

SIGNING TIPS

To get someone's attention, you can tap them on the
shoulder, wave your hand in their peripheral vision, or move
into their line of vision and sign "excuse me" by brushing
your fingertips off your upturned palm.

Don't shout! Keep your hands near your chest
and keep your arm movements small.

---

light/bright/clear

Begin with Flat O hands together in front of your body, then move your hands up and out while opening to 5 hands.

cold/winter

Shake S hands, as if you are cold.

hot

Twist a Bent 5 hand out from your mouth.

tree

Rest the elbow of your upright right arm on your left palm and twist your arm back and forth a few times. You can sign **forest** by moving your arms to the right while you sign **tree**.

flower

Place a Flat O hand at one side of your nose, then move your hand to the other side.

Earth

Place the thumb and middle finger of your right hand on the back of your left hand and rock your right hand up and down.

grass

Brush the palm of a Bent 5 hand against your chin twice.

summer

Wipe your index finger across your forehead while changing to an X hand.

spring

Push your right Flat O hand up through your left C hand and open your right hand.

fall/autumn

Brush your left elbow with an Open B hand.

PRACTICE SENTENCES

1. Let's climb a tree.

you-and-me

climb

tree

2. How's the weather?

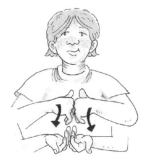

how

weather

today

3. It's cold in here!

cold

4. I love summer.

me

love

summer

5. The sky is cloudy today.

sky   cloud   today

16

IT'S PARTY TIME!
Party Signs

Host a sign language party and have everybody join in the fun.

party

Swing P hands back and forth.

celebrate

Circle a Baby O hand above your shoulder.

birthday

Place an Open B hand on your chest, bring your hand down to land in your other palm, and then sign **day**.

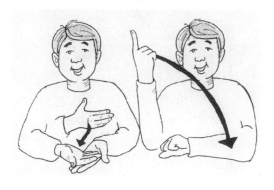

surprise

Place Baby O hands at your temples and flick up your index fingers.

sleepover

Sign **sleep** and then sign **party**.

barbecue

Fingerspell B-B-Q

decorate

Move Bent 5 hands in small circles in front of your face.

balloon

Hold S hands at your mouth, one in front of the other, then move your hands out to the side as you open to C hands.

invite

Sweep an Open B hand in toward your body.

soda/pop

Place the middle finger of your right Open 8 hand in your left S hand, lift up your right hand, open it, and bring it down on your left hand.

pizza

Draw a Z with a Bent V hand and then close to an A hand.

cake

Slide a C hand down an Open B hand.

candy

Twist an index finger at the side of your chin.

candles

Place the index finger of your right hand at your lips, move it to the palm of your left 5 hand, and wiggle your left fingers.

prize/gift/present

Arc Baby O hands forward.

game

Tap the knuckles of your Open A hands together.

time

Tap your right index finger on
your left arm.

PRACTICE SENTENCES

1. Happy birthday!

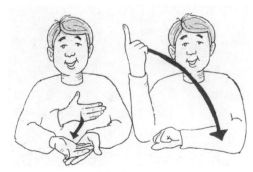

happy   birthday

2. It's party time!

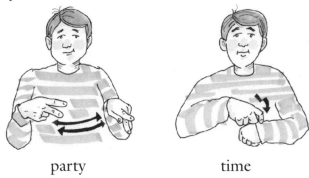

party　　　　　time

3. Do you want more cake and ice cream?

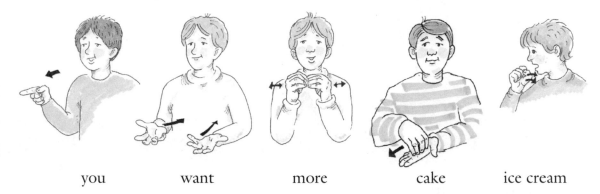

you　　　　want　　　　more　　　　cake　　　　ice cream

4. How many did you invite?

how-many　　　　　　you　　　　　　invite

5. My favorite candy is chocolate.

my   favorite   candy   chocolate

17

FAMILY AND FRIENDS
People Signs

Greet your family and friends in sign language, then teach them how to sign, too!

people

Loop P hands forward in
alternating circles.

father

Tap the thumb of a 5 hand on
your forehead.

mother

Tap the thumb of a 5 hand on
your chin.

grandmother

Sign **mother**, then bounce your
hand forward twice.

grandfather

Sign **father**, then bounce your hand forward twice.

boy

Place the thumb of a C hand on your forehead, then pull your hand out and close it to a Flat O.

girl

Place the thumb of an A hand on your cheek and stroke it forward and down.

brother

Sign **boy**, then bring your hand down, changing to a 1 hand, to meet your other 1 hand.

baby

Place your right arm in your left arm and rock your arms back and forth, as if cradling a baby.

sister

Sign **girl**, then bring your hand down, changing to a 1 hand, to meet your other 1 hand.

SIGNING TIP

Deaf people make up name signs for each other
so they can easily refer to someone without having to
spell the full name. Most name signs use the handshape for
the first letter of the name, and they often represent a physical
characteristic or a person's personality. For example, the name
sign for a girl named Rebecca who has long hair might be
the sign **long hair** made with an R. The name sign for
a boy named Matt might be an M near the temple,
where the sign **boy** is made.

kid

Put the index finger of a 1 hand under your nose and twist your hand.

parents

Begin with the middle finger of a P hand on the side of your chin, then move your hand up to the side of your forehead.

family

Hold the thumbs of your F hands together, then circle your hands around until your pinky fingers touch.

friend

Link the index fingers of your X hands, then separate your hands, twist them around, and relink your index fingers.

best friend

link your index fingers and move
your hands forward.

you

Point your index finger forward
toward an imaginary person.

your

Push an Open B hand out toward
an imaginary person.

I/me

Point an index finger at yourself.

my/mine

Place an Open B hand on your chest.

it

Point your index finger toward an imaginary object.

PRACTICE SENTENCES

1. My mother is a teacher.

my

mother

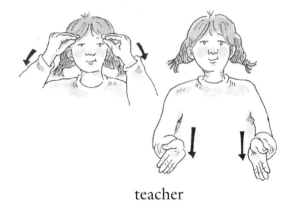

teacher

2. Is he your brother?

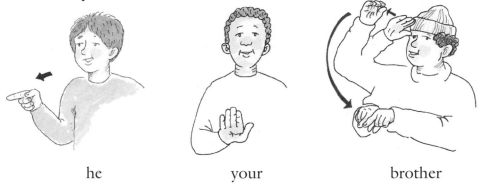

he   your   brother

3. Is your cat a boy or a girl?

your   cat   boy   girl

4. You are my best friend.

you   my   best-friend

5. My parents went on vacation.

my   parents   go   vacation

6. I love your family.

me   love   your   family

18

HERE AND THERE
Place Signs

Tell your friends where you have been and where you are going with these place signs!

place

Hold P hands out in front of your
body, with your middle fingers
touching, then circle your hands
back until middle fingers touch
again.

Washington, D.C.

Place a W hand on your shoulder,
circle it outward twice, then
fingerspell D-C.

California

Touch your ear with your index finger, then move your hand down, changing to a Y hand, and wiggle it a little.

New York

Brush a Y hand back and forth on your other palm.

ocean

Sign **water**, then open your hands and roll them forward in waves.

beach

Hold one arm flat and wave the other hand forward and back toward your arm, like waves hitting a beach.

mountain

Tap one A hand on top of the other A hand, then open your hands and glide them upward in waves.

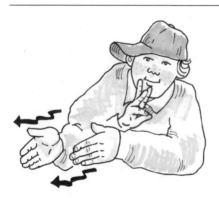

river

Sign **water**, then glide Open B hands forward with palms facing each other.

lake

Sign **water**, then open your hand and circle it around.

camp

Hold V hands in front of your body, with fingers touching, then move your hands down and apart.

city

Tap the fingers of your Open B hands together twice while moving your hands to the right.

state

Place an S hand at the top of your upright palm, then bounce your hand down to the bottom of your palm.

country

Circle a Y hand around your elbow.

America

Interlock your fingers and circle your hands around.

north

Move an N hand straight up.

south

Move an S hand straight down.

east

Move an E hand to the right.

west

Move a W hand to the left.

PRACTICE SENTENCES

1. My house is in California.

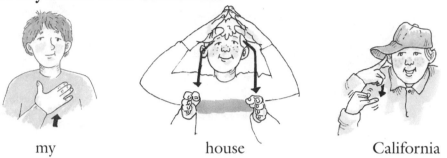

my house California

2. My family is going camping.

my family go camp

3. Should we go north or south?

you-and-me go north south

4. My favorite place is the beach.

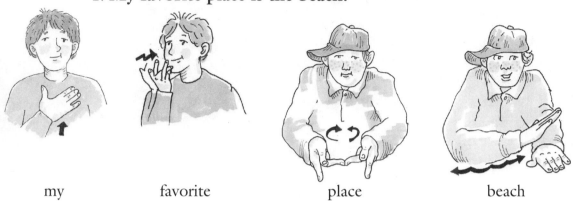

| my | favorite | place | beach |

5. Is that a lake or a river?

| that | lake | river |

6. I am an American.

| me | America | person |

19

LET'S PLAY
Play Signs

It's fun to play around with sign language!

play

Twist Y hands in front of your body.

toy

Shake T hands.

fun

Move an H hand from your nose down to rest on the fingers of your other H hand.

bicycle

Circle S hands forward, alternating hands as if pedaling.

doll

Place the index finger of an X hand on your nose and move it down.

ball

Form a circle with your hands and tap fingertips together.

When you reach the end of a fingerspelled word, pause for half a second, but don't drop your hand, and then keep going.

When spelling a word that contains double letters (like *bottle* or *doll*), you can make a small bounce, sign the letter twice, or glide the letter to the side a little.

kite

Pretend to hold a kite string with both hands and move your hands up and down.

puzzle

Place fingertips of Flat O hands together and twist hands in opposite directions.

video game

Place a V hand on top of the fingertips of your other hand, move the V forward in a circle and end with a T hand on your palm; then change to 10 hands and knock your knuckles together.

chase

Place one A hand behind the other A hand, then move your hands forward with the back hand moving in small circles.

jump rope

Circle both hands forward, as if you are jumping rope.

hopscotch

Put an upside-down V hand on your other palm, then lift your hand and bend your V fingers twice.

playground

Sign **play**, then rub your fingertips together.

PRACTICE SENTENCES

1. Let's play ball.

you-and-me   play   ball

2. Do you want to fly a kite?

you   want   kite

3. I made this doll.

me   make   this   doll

4. Did you ride your bike here?

you   bike   here

5. Stop chasing me!

stop   chase   me

6. Jumping rope is fun!

jump rope   fun

20

SCARED STIFF
Scary Signs

Don't be afraid—these signs aren't scary. They're fun!

scared/afraid

Hold A hands below your shoulders, then move them toward each other while opening your hands.

fear/afraid

Hold 5 hands, palms in, in front of your chest and slide them back and forth in short movements.

danger/dangerous

Place your right A hand below your left A hand, and brush your right thumb up the back of your left hand twice.

scream

Hold a Bent 5 hand at your mouth, raise your arm in a long movement, and twist your hand around.

shock

Hold S hands over your eyes, then open your hands to C hands.

horror

Hold 5 hands, palms out, at either side of your face; shake them slightly and look scared.

nightmare

Begin with the fingertips of a B hand at your lips, then twist your hand out and down (**bad**); next, place your index finger on your forehead and bend it repeatedly as you pull it out and up.

dead

Hold one hand palm up and the other one palm down, and turn both hands over.

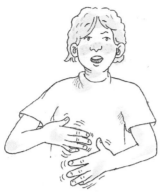

nervous

Hold 5 hands in front of your chest and shake them as if you are nervous.

ghost/spirit

Place the fingertips of one Open 8 hand above the fingertips of the other Open 8 hand, then pull hands apart while closing thumbs and middle fingers.

skeleton

Cross Bent V hands at the wrists in front of your neck and tap wrists together twice.

witch

Place the index finger of an X hand on your nose, then move it down to land on the index finger of your other X hand.

monster

Hold Bent 5 hands out and make a scary face.

bury/grave/cemetery

Hold Bent B hands out in front of you, then arc them back toward your chest.

PRACTICE SENTENCES

1. You scared me!

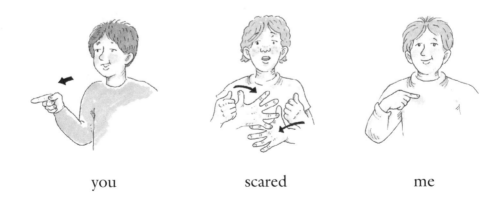

| you | scared | me |

2. I'm going to be a witch for Halloween.

me   witch   Halloween

3. There's a monster in my room.

monster   my   room.

4. Are you nervous in a cemetery?

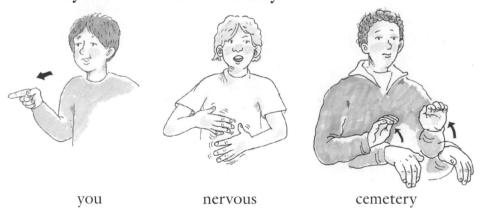

you   nervous   cemetery

21

IS IT RECESS YET?
School Signs

Here are some signs to make school more fun!

school

Tap Open B hands together twice.

learn

Place the fingertips of your right hand on your left palm, then pull your right hand up to your forehead while closing it to a Flat O hand.

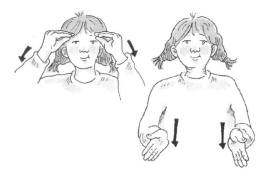

teacher

Move Flat O hands out from forehead and sign **person**.

student

Sign **learn** and then sign **person**.

book

Hold palms together and open them, like opening a book.

paper

Brush the heels of your palms together twice.

homework

Place a Flat O hand on your cheek, bring your hand down while changing to an S hand, and tap it on top of your other S hand twice.

recess

Link X hands and pull them up.

class

Hold C hands out so thumbs touch, then circle hands around until pinkies touch.

pencil

Begin with a Baby O hand at your mouth, bring your hand down, and brush it across your open palm.

desk/table

Place one arm on top of the other arm and tap arms together twice.

social studies

Bounce an S hand in a small arc to the side.

English

Place one hand over the other hand and pull your hands toward you.

poetry

Wave a P hand in front of your extended arm.

SIGNING TIPS

Practice reading fingerspelled words in syllables, not as individual letters. Sound the words out as you spell them and read them. Soon you will be able to read the words automatically.

Practice fingerspelling throughout the day.
Soon you will become faster and smoother.

---

math

Brush M hands against each other twice.

science

Turn Open A hands upside down and circle them alternately, as if mixing chemicals.

history

Shake an H hand up and down.

language

Hold L hands face down and wiggle them apart.

art

Wiggle the pinky of an I hand down your palm, as if drawing.

PE

Fingerspell P-E.

library

Circle an L in the air.

number

Place fingertips of Flat O hands together and rotate hands.

restroom

Bounce an R hand in a small arc to the side.

test/exam

Hold up X hands, circle them around, as if making a question mark, and then open your hands.

PRACTICE SENTENCES

1. What school do you go to?

| what | school | you | go |

2. I hate homework!

me   hate   homework

3. I love my teacher!

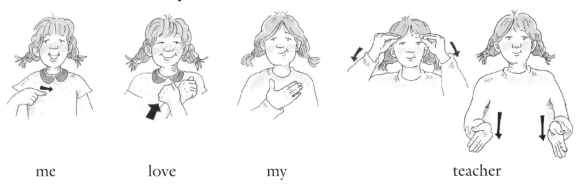

me   love   my   teacher

4. Math is my favorite class.

math   my   favorite   class

5. Do you have my book?

you   have   my   book

6. We had an English test today.

we   had   English   test   today

22

LET'S GO SHOPPING
Shopping Signs

Take your signs along on your next shopping trip.

store/sale/sell

Hold Flat O hands down, then raise them up twice for **store**, once for **sale** and **sell**.

buy/purchase

Place a Flat O hand in your other palm, then lift your Flat O hand up and forward in an arc.

pay

Place the tip of the index finger of a 1 hand on your other palm and brush your index finger forward.

cost/price

Brush an X hand across your other palm.

cheap

Brush an Open B hand across the other Open B hand.

money

Tap the back of a Flat O hand on your other palm.

wallet

Place palms together, then separate your hands, leaving fingertips touching.

dollar

Place your right hand around the fingers of your left Open B hand and slide your right hand off your left hand.

credit card

Brush an upright A hand back and forth along your other palm.

cents

Place the tip of an index finger on your forehead and pull your hand straight out.

PRACTICE SENTENCES

1. How much does that cost?

how-much

that

cost

2. The food was cheap.

food   cheap

3. This is my mom's credit card.

this   my   mother   credit card

4. I want to buy a shirt.

me   want   buy   shirt

176   LET'S GO SHOPPING

5. There is no money in my wallet!

no   money   my   wallet

6. Let's go to the shoe store.

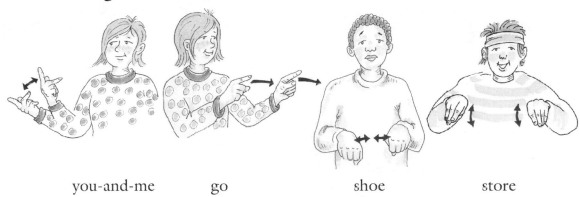

you-and-me   go   shoe   store

23

LET'S GO!
Travel Signs

If you're planning to take a trip, watch for "signs" as you go!

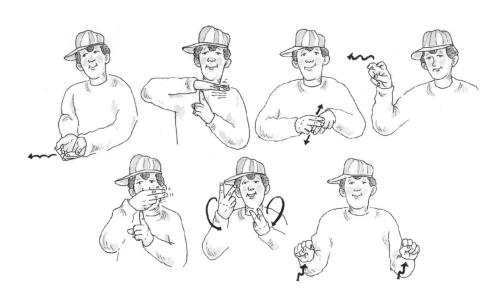

travel/trip
Zigzag a Bent V hand forward.

airplane/fly
Extend your thumb, index finger, and pinky, then fly your hand through the air, once for **fly**, twice for **airplane**.

boat
Cup your hands together like the shape of a boat and bounce them forward.

car/automobile
Pretend to turn the wheel of a car with S hands.

helicopter

Place an Open B hand on top of your index finger and flutter your fingers.

motorcycle

Hold S hands out, as if gripping handlebars, and twist them up twice.

SIGNING TIPS

If a phrase is plural, such as "three cats," sign the number first. You can also make the sign **cat** two times.

If a verb and a noun have a related meaning—like *fly* and *airplane*, *sit* and *chair,* and *print* and *newspaper*—sign the verb with one movement and the noun with two movements.

train

Place the fingers of one H hand across the fingers of your other H hand and slide the top fingers back and forth twice.

ticket

Slide Bent V fingers into the edge of an Open B hand twice.

subway

Sign **train**, then slide your index finger under your other hand.

visit
Alternate circling V hands outward.

hotel
Place an H hand on the index finger of a 1 hand and bend your H fingers twice.

PRACTICE SENTENCES

1. Let's go on the train.

| you-and-me | go | train |

2. Did you come here by airplane?

you   fly   here

3. Is that your car?

that   your   car

4. We're going on a trip north.

you-and-me   go   trip   north

5. That's a big boat!

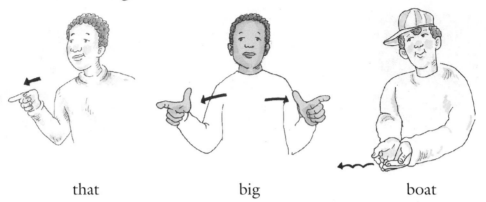

that	big	boat

6. I'm going to visit my grandmother.

me	visit	my	grandmother

24

EXTRA FUN SIGNS

Here are some other signs you'll need to have fun with sign language.

wow

Hold W hands on either side of your face, bend your fingers down and up twice, and form an O with your mouth.

wow/that's amazing

Shake a Bent B hand up and down twice.

dream

Place your index finger on your forehead, then wiggle it as you pull your hand out and up.

cool/fine

Place the thumb of a 5 hand on your chest and wiggle your fingers.

whisper

Place a Bent 5 hand around your mouth.

stubborn

Place the thumbs of Open B hands at your temples and bend your hands down.

secret/private

Tap the thumb of an A hand on your lips.

crabby/mad

Hold a Bent 5 hand in front of your face and bend your fingers rapidly.

funny

Brush your nose twice with your index and middle fingers.

favorite/prefer

Tap the middle finger of an Open 8 hand on your chin twice.

disappear

Pull a 5 hand down inside your other palm, and close it to a Flat O hand.

fight

Brush S hands past each other.

okay
Fingerspell O-K.

yes
Nod an S hand up and down.

no
Close your index and middle fingers to your thumb.

question mark
Draw a question mark in the air with your index finger.

huh?

Bounce an X hand up and down while bending your index finger.

what's up?

Place the middle fingers of Open 8 hands on your chest, then arc your hands up and out.

crazy

Make small circles at the side of your head with your index finger.

joke

Brush an X hand down your nose twice.

stupid/dumb

Tap your forehead with an S hand.

strange/weird

Move a C hand across your face and bend it down.

cartoon

Brush your nose with a C hand twice.

silly/foolish

Wave a Y hand back and forth in front of your nose.

like

Place your middle finger and
thumb on your chest, then
pull your hand out and bring
your middle finger and thumb
together.

PRACTICE SENTENCES

1. Wow! That's cool!

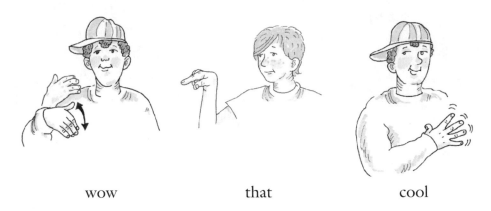

wow   that   cool

2. I had a weird dream.

me   have   weird   dream

3. You're so silly.

you   silly

4. Do you want a drink?

you   want   drink   question

5. Let's not fight.

you me (shake your head no) + fight

6. I like to watch cartoons.

me like watch cartoons

SIGN LANGUAGE GAMES AND ACTIVITIES

1. Alphabet Sign

Level:
Easy

Number of Players:
2 or more

How to Play:

1. Players sit in a circle.
2. First player signs a word that begins with the letter A, such as "apple." Correct signs earn one point.
3. Next player signs a word that begins with the letter B.
4. Continue through the alphabet, signing words to match the letters.
5. If a player can't think of a sign that begins with the correct letter, and another player comes up with a sign, the player who couldn't think of a sign loses a point.

2. Bad Words

Level:
Easy

Number of Players
2 or more

How to Play:

1. The first player chooses a common word to avoid, such as "the" or "and."
2. The players have a conversation in sign language without using the selected word.
3. If a player accidentally uses the word, she loses a point.
4. After a few minutes, the players select a new word to avoid and play again.

5. Option: Play the game by fingerspelling sentences, while avoiding a selected letter.

3. Body Language

Level: **Number of Players:**
Easy   2 or more

How to Play:

1. Photocopy the vocabulary words in the index.

2. Cut out the words and place them in a stack.

3. Player picks a word and must act out the word with gestures, without using ASL signs.

4. Others must try to guess the word.

5. Take turns drawing and acting out the words.

4. Combine a Sign

Level: **Number of Players:**
Easy   2 or more

How to Play:

1. Photocopy the vocabulary words in the index.

2. Cut out the words and place them in a stack.

3. Player picks two words and must sign them together.

4. Other players must try to guess both signs.

5. Finger Fun

Level:
Easy

Number of Players:
2 or more

How to Play:

1. Player uses only his fingers—no signs—to act out a story. For example, he might have two fingers walk up and ask the other two fingers to dance.

2. Have the other players guess what's happening in the story.

3. Take turns telling stories with your fingers.

6. Fishy Signs

Level:
Easy

Number of Players
2 or more

How to Play:

1. Play the card game "Fish" in sign language.

2. If anyone talks by mistake, they lose a turn or a card.

7. Funny Feelings

Level:
Easy

Number of Players:
2 or more

How to Play:

1. First player chooses one of the feeling words below and acts it out without talking.

2. Other players try to guess the feeling.

3. Players take turns expressing feelings without words.

happy	excited	fearful
shy	scared	guilty
distracted	jealous	nervous
depressed	panicked	shocked
snobby	upset	sad
queasy	silly	bored
curious	crazy	

8. Gesture Guess

Level:
Easy

Number of Players:
2 or more

How to Play:

1. Player spots an object in the room, and then shapes it with her hands.

2. Other players try to guess what the object is.

9. Liar, Liar?

Level:
Easy

Number of Players:
2 or more

How to Play:

1. The first player signs something that may or may not be true.

2. Other players must guess if he's telling the truth or lying by watching his facial expression and body language.

3. When everyone has guessed, the player confesses whether his statement was true or false.

4. The players who guessed correctly get a point.

10. Hand Shapes

Level:
Easy

Number of players:
2 or more

How to Play:

1. The first player forms the first letter of the alphabet with both hands. Then she must act out an action to match her hand-shapes. For example, if her hands are shaped like the letter A, she might pretend to drive a car, or put up her fists for a fight.

2. Other players must guess what she's acting out.

3. Players take turns as they continue through the alphabet.

11. Mime, No Sign

Level:
Easy

Number of Players:
2 or more

How to Play:

1. The first player acts out a scene from her life but can't use any real signs.

2. Other players try to guess what the scene is.

3. Award points to players who guess correctly.

4. Players take turns miming and guessing.

12. No-Sign Charades

Level:
Easy

Number of Players:
4 or more

How to Play:

1. Players divide into two teams.

2. Each team writes down movie, song, or book titles on pieces of paper, folds the papers, and places them in a bowl.

3. A player from one team picks a slip of paper from the other team's bowl and must act out the title for her team, without using signs or voice, only gestures and body language.

13. Tongue Tied

Level:
Easy

Number of Players:
2 or more

How to Play:

1. Spend a half-hour not talking or signing, just communicating with gestures, facial expressions, and so on.

2. Players then talk about their conversation to see if they really understood each other.

14. Signo Bingo

Level:
Easy

Number of Players:
2 or more

How to Play:

1. Make bingo cards, five squares across by five squares down.

2. Photocopy the manual alphabet and cut out the letters.

3. Glue the letters onto the bingo cards in a random order.

4. Cut out another set of letters and stack them in a pile.

5. Take turns picking a card.

6. Sign the letter on the card and have everyone place a bean or coin on the square if the letter matches.

7. The first player to fill five squares in a row—up, down, or diagonally—wins the game.

8. Shuffle the deck and play again.

15. Sign Buzz

Level:
Easy

Number of Players:
3 or more

How to Play:

1. Sit in a circle.

2. The first player begins counting in sign language, by signing the number 1.

3. The next player signs 2, and so on, until a player reaches a number that has a seven or adds up to seven. Then he must fingerspell the word "buzz" instead of signing the number.

4. If a player makes a mistake, he's out of the game or loses a point.

16. Signing Hangman

Level: **Number of Players:**
Easy   2 or more

How to Play:

1. Play Hangman by guessing fingerspelled letters.
2. When a player knows the word, he has to sign it.

17. Spelling Search

Level: **Number of Players:**
Easy   2 or more

How to Play:

1. One player spots something in the room and fingerspells the first letter of the word.
2. The other players try to guess what the object is, using signs or fingerspelling.
3. If they can't guess, the player fingerspells another letter in the word, in any order.
4. The first player to guess the word wins the game.

18. Sign Stunts

Level:
Intermediate

Number of Players:
2 or more

How to Play:

1. The first player makes a sign and then must do something else with that sign. For example, if the player signs **ball**, she could use her hands to pick something up or put a crown on her head.

2. Take turns making signs and using them in some other way.

19. Comical Sign

Level:
Intermediate

Number of Players:
2 or more

How to Play:

1. Cut out comic strips from the newspaper or comic books.

2. Give a strip to each player.

3. Take turns signing the dialogue as you act out the scene.

4. See how many players can guess what the comic strip is about.

20. Get the Joke

Level:
Intermediate

Number of Players:
2 or more

How to Play:

1. Get a joke book from the library or bookstore.

2. Players take turns telling each other jokes using sign language and fingerspelling.

21. Ghost Guess

Level:
Intermediate

Number of Players:
3 or more

How to Play:

1. Play "Ghost" using fingerspelling, by taking turns spelling words one letter at a time. The object is to avoid being the player who says the last letter of the word.
2. The first player fingerspells a letter.
3. The next player thinks of a word that starts with that letter and fingerspells the second letter in the word.
4. Each player adds a letter.
5. The first person to spell a complete word with at least 3 letters loses the round and gets a "G."
6. Each time a player loses a round, he gets another letter in the word "ghost."
7. The first person to get all five letters, G-H-O-S-T, loses the game.

22. Giant Sign

Level:
Intermediate

Number of Players:
2 or more

How to Play:

1. A player thinks of a sentence to say in sign language. Then,

the player signs the sentence but must exaggerate the signs to make them extra large.

2. The other players try to guess what is being signed.

23. Deaf-initions

Level:
Intermediate

Number of Players:
4 or more

How to Play:

1. Players sit at a table with a dictionary.

2. The first player finds a word in the dictionary that he doesn't know and fingerspells the word to the other players.

3. Other players must make up a definition and write it down.

4. The first player reads all the definitions, along with the real definition, and the other players try to guess the real definition.

5. Players get points for guessing the right definition and for fooling the other players.

6. Players take turns choosing words and guessing definitions.

24. Find a Sign

Level:
Intermediate

Number of Players:
2 or more

How to Play:

1. Photocopy two sets of 20 signs in the book.

2. Cut them out, mix them up, and lay them out face down on the table.

3. Players take turns flipping over signs two at a time to try to find a match.

4. Each time a player gets a match, she gets another turn. Otherwise, the next player gets a turn.

5. The player with the most pairs wins the game.

25. Match Signs

Level:
Intermediate

Number of Players:
3 or more

How to Play:

1. One player chooses a category from the list below.

2. The other players sign or fingerspell words in the category as fast as they can in one minute, while the first player writes them down on paper.

3. The player who signs the most words in the category wins the round.

4. Players take turns choosing categories and signing words.

fast foods	school subjects	boys' names
girls' names	cars	traffic signs
rock stars	clothing	baby items
plants	trees	cartoon characters
movie stars	candy bars	desserts
colors	furniture	cities
TV shows	animals	

26. No Talking!

Level:
Intermediate

Number of Players:
2 or more

How to Play:

1. Players see how long they can communicate with one another in sign language without saying a word.

2. The first player to accidentally talk loses a point.

27. Number It

Level:
Intermediate

Number of Players:
2 or more

How to Play:

1. The first player makes the sign for the number 1, and then must use that handshape to make another sign. For example, he might sign **up**, **go**, or **crazy**.

2. The next player makes a sign using the number 2.

3. Players continue taking turns using the numbers from 1 to 10.

28. Oppo-Sign

Level:
Intermediate

Number of Players:
2 or more

How to Play:

1. The first player signs a word that has an opposite, such as **up** or **happy**.

2. The other players must sign the opposite word, such as **down** or **sad**.

3. If there are more than 2 players, the first player to come up with the opposite sign wins a point.

4. Players take turns signing words that have opposites.

29. Read My Lips

Level:
Intermediate

Number of Players:
2 or more

How to Play:

1. Have a conversation without talking or signing, just by reading lips.

2. See how well you can understand one another and how many mistakes you made!

30. Secret Sign

Level:
Intermediate

Number of Players:
6 or more

How to Play:

1. Players sit in a circle.

2. First player signs a sentence to the second player without the other players watching.

3. The second player signs that same sentence to the next player, and so on, until all the players have seen the sentence, one at a time.

4. The last player signs the sentence to everyone to see if it's the same sentence the first player signed.

31. See and Sign

Level:
Intermediate

Number of Players:
4 or more

How to Play:

1. Players sit in a circle.

2. First player signs a word.

3. Second player signs that same word, then adds another word.

4. Next player signs both words in order, then adds another word.

5. Continue repeating signs and adding new words as you move around the circle.

6. If a player can't remember all the signs in order, he loses the game.

32. Sign-a-Rhyme

Level:
Intermediate

Number of Players:
2 or more

How to Play:

1. The first player signs the first line of a rhyme, such as "Roses are red, Violets are blue," or "I met a man named Mike."

2. The second player must sign a sentence related to the first

sentence and it must rhyme, such as "I like to sign, and so do you," or "He liked to take a hike."

3. Keep going until you run out of rhymes, then begin a new rhyme.

33. Sign-a-Sentence

Level:
Intermediate

Number of Players:
2 or more

How to Play:

1. One player signs a word of his choice.

2. The other player must use the sign in a sentence.

3. Take turns signing words and sentences.

4. Make the game more challenging by adding two or three words for the same sentence.

34. Sign-a-Song

Level:
Intermediate

Number of Players:
2 or more

How to Play:

1. Write down lyrics to a favorite song.

2. Learn the signs and practice the song without music.

3. Sign the song along to the music.

4. Give a performance for family and friends.

5. Videotape yourself and play it back.

35. Sign Morph

Level:
Intermediate

Number of Players:
2 or more

How to Play:

1. Think of a two-word phrase, such as "sick man" or "yellow plane."
2. Sign the words smoothly together so they morph into each other.
3. See if the other players can understand your morphed signs.

36. Sign Language Theater

Level:
Intermediate

Number of Player:
2 or more

How to Play:

1. Write a play or read a simple story book.
2. Act out the story using gestures and sign language.
3. Videotape your performance and play it back.

37. Snap and Sign

Level:
Intermediate

Number of Players:
2 or more

How to Play:

1. Sit in a circle with your legs crossed.

2. Choose a category, such as candy bars, animals, and so on.

3. To begin, players slap their knees, clap their hands, then one player signs a word from the category.

4. Keep the slapping and clapping going in rhythm, going around the circle as you take turns signing related words.

5. The first person who can't come up with a sign loses a point.

6. Change categories and keep playing.

38. Story Sign

Level:
Intermediate

Number of Players:
2 or more

How to Play:

1. The first player starts a story in sign.

2. The next player continues the story, also in sign.

3. Players continue adding sentences until the story comes to an end.

4. Another player begins a new story in sign.

39. Sign or Dare

Level:
Intermediate

Number of Players:
2 or more

How to Play:

1. Take turns signing the Sign or Dare questions below.

2. If a player does not want to answer with the truth, in sign language, she must do one of the dares listed below.

Truth Questions

- What is your best characteristic?
- If you won a million dollars, what would you do with it?
- Which movie star would you like to kiss?
- What did you look like on your worst day?
- What secret did you accidentally spill?
- Which movie star does each player look like?
- Which player tells the worst jokes?
- If you could change your name, what would it be?
- What kind of animals do the other players remind you of?
- If you had one hour to live, what would you do?
- What's your favorite age and why?
- What's your biggest fear?
- What is your worst habit?
- What have you borrowed and not returned?

Dare Cards

- Do the moonwalk.
- Imitate your favorite animal.
- Demonstrate a karate move, even if you don't know one.
- Pretend you see a monster.
- Sing "Happy Birthday" in sign.
- Make the player next to you laugh in 30 seconds.
- Draw a face on your tummy and make it "talk."
- Act like a pig.
- Act out your Academy Award acceptance speech.
- Act out a fashion show runway walk.

40. Twenty People Questions

Level:
Intermediate

Number of Players:
2 or more

How to Play:

1. One player thinks of a famous person or character (see suggestions below).
2. The other players take turns guessing who it is using sign language.
3. The first player to guess wins the game.
4. Another player thinks of a person and the game continues.

Bugs Bunny	Frankenstein	Justin Timberlake
Barney the Dinosaur	Mickey Mouse	Superman
Big Bird	Peter Pan	Nemo
Harriet the Spy	Dr. Seuss	The President
Garfield the Cat	The Lion King	Harry Potter
Queen Elizabeth	Mary Kate and Ashley	Rugrats
SpongeBob	George Washington	

41. Who Am I?

Level:
Intermediate

Number of Players:
2 or more

How to Play:

1. Tape the name of a famous person on players' backs.
2. Players must sign questions to each other until they guess who they are.

42. Speed Sign

Level:
Advanced

Number of Players:
2 or more

How to Play:

1. Practice signing a poem or song.

2. Use a timer and sign the poem or song as fast as you can.

3. Check the timer to see who signed the fastest.

4. See if you can improve your time.

43. Touch and Tell

Level:
Advanced

Number of Players:
2 or more

How to Play:

1. The first player closes his eyes.

2. The next player fingerspells words in the first player's palm.

3. The player tries to read the words in his palm.

Glossary &
Resources

GLOSSARY

Here are some helpful vocabulary words related to sign language and deafness.

American Sign Language/ASL: a distinct visual language used by Deaf people. ASL has its own vocabulary, grammar, and syntax.

Deaf: a severe or profound hearing loss.

Deaf community: a group of people who share a common culture that may include deafness, ASL, and certain beliefs, goals, and experiences.

Fingerspelling/Manual alphabet: signs that represent each letter of the alphabet.

Gesture: a motion that is commonly understood by most people.

Hard of Hearing: a mild or moderate hearing loss.

Interpreter: a person who translates speech into sign and vice versa.

Lipreading/Speechreading: watching the formation of words on the lips to communicate.

Total Communication: the use of various forms of communication, including sign language, fingerspelling, speechreading, gestures, facial expressions, and voice.

RESOURCES

Here are some internet sites where you can find more information on sign language and deafness.

http://babel.uoregon.edu/yamada/fonts/asl.html: download your own fingerspelling fonts

www.deafness.about.com/cs/signfeats2/a/signdictionary: online sign dictionary

www.handspeak.com: online sign dictionary, stories, articles

www.kidsdomain.com/kids/links/Sign_Language.html: lessons for learning sign

www.lessontutor.com/ASLgenhome.html: lessons for learning sign

www.masterstech-home.com/asldict.html: online sign language dictionary

www.surfnetkids.com/signlanguage.htm: sign language sites for kids

Index